UNCOLLECTED LATER POEMS (1968–1979)

WAVE BOOKS / SEATTLE AND NEW YORK

ERNST MEISTER
UNCOLLECTED
LATER POEMS
(1968–1979)

TRANSLATED BY
GRAHAM FOUST AND
SAMUEL FREDERICK

PUBLISHED BY WAVE BOOKS

WWW.WAVEPOETRY.COM

ENGLISH TRANSLATION COPYRIGHT © 2023

BY GRAHAM FOUST AND SAMUEL FREDERICK

WAVE BOOKS TITLES ARE DISTRIBUTED TO THE TRADE BY
CONSORTIUM BOOK SALES AND DISTRIBUTION

PHONE: 800-283-3572 / SAN 631-760X

LIBRARY OF CONGRESS CATALOGING-IN-PUBLICATION DATA

NAMES: MEISTER, ERNST, 1911–1979, AUTHOR.

FOUST, GRAHAM W., 1970–TRANSLATOR.

FREDERICK, SAMUEL, TRANSLATOR.

TITLE: UNCOLLECTED LATER POEMS (1968–1979) / ERNST MEISTER ;
TRANSLATED BY GRAHAM FOUST AND SAMUEL FREDERICK.

DESCRIPTION: SEATTLE : WAVE BOOKS, [2023]

IDENTIFIERS: LCCN 2023009950 | ISBN 9781950268894 (PAPERBACK)

SUBJECTS: LCSH: MEISTER, ERNST, 1911–1979—
TRANSLATIONS INTO ENGLISH. | LCGFT: POETRY.

CLASSIFICATION: LCC PT2625.E3224 U53 2023

DDC 831/.914—DC23/ENG/20230306

LC RECORD AVAILABLE AT HTTPS://LCCN.LOC.GOV/2023009950

DESIGNED BY CRISIS

PRINTED IN THE UNITED STATES OF AMERICA

9 8 7 6 5 4 3 2 1

FIRST EDITION

UNCOLLECTED LATER POEMS (1968—1979)

In the winds—
those of the astonished
morning especially—
there can be
cunning
and it can make blissful
he who is familiar
with fate.

Now the leaves
at your door
flicker right before
my eyes,
and small shadows
play fro and to
on the wall.

Sometimes
love comes
to an end.

1968

With one of those
poor ships
upward
I pushed myself
to set foot on
the desolate moon.

Sat down there
and wrote
figures
from Earth's knowledge
in the alien dust.

And
a long ruminating,
crooked
under the silence,
she who checks your
hesitating fingers.

1968

Where

moreover

what's high climbs

above what's highest,

and is

an icy head,

not blindable by suns—

the heavens.

But even here,

where, near the earth,

legend comes

from the poem,

flowers and grasses

are, like that head,

unthinking.

1968

Exactly as
thoughts, thoughts
that scarcely
tear
the girl's silk,
the fleeting storms
don't tear the sky.

Water falls
like lead
into the water
of the well in front of the house.

1968

Through door
and window
sheer wind.
The delicate
shadow of the body
flies away,
toward you,
you naked
dogs on the
barren slopes.

Go ahead and hunt
and howl,
here
I'm resting
a farewell,
here here, where I
was last.

Beautifully, by day
a giant mountain
is out there.

Yet, however one
takes it,
that's not
much.

1968

But what passed
was over
and over
passed.

For then namely
the name of each comes
into appearance,
then namely
the light shines as
what is astonishingly originated.

Then namely also
suffering,
the most thorough
moves into the light of day.

1969

LITTLE MONOPOD

I had two parents and two legs too.
Parents always come in twos.
The war tore one of my legs in two.
My parents were also there.
Boom! Nothing spared!
Now I stand alone on one leg.

I often crutch to the cemetery,
where my parents lie buried,
because there I'm not so sad;
I practice crutchless jumps
at their final spot.
My parents like this a lot.

Then when I crutch back home
I pluck a flower from the tomb.
I take just one,
so as not to be so alone.

1969

(Death)
From there,
out of the organs' decay,
the carcass of every human,
I came to you
in the chattel of time.

Our body,
hair and face
mirrored one another.

You beauty.

I also want to turn and look
from that place
of the heard sea,
for the sake of the world's
light,
toward others' talk.

1969

It is,
due to the circumstance of things—
circuitousness, a kind—
not at all singable; but now
I sing:

You hold
in your hand
a sphere—that is
my love,
and I
hold in my hand
a sphere—
that is your love.

That seems enough.

Nonetheless, tell
our father, the weaver,
he should, since he is certainly
able, moved by

longing,
make a knot
out of both our faces,
so that the long thread shortens,
pulled at its ends
around the one and around the other
righteous house.

1969

The tip of the stalk
draws
the tossed flower—
where is it?

Something gets misplaced
out of guilt.

What's far removed
shows
her, the uneasy sleeper
in broad daylight.

I know talk
behind the courage
and the muteness,
the false one, before it.

I don't
want to hear anything
about storytelling.

1969

To allegorical birds
I am
branches.

It's crows.
I hear
them say, the air
in the vastness spins
the end of the song.

But while they
nod and think that
everything escapes,
I see
a golden crocheting
around their talons.

1969

Word,
whose sound
ends in the throat.
You don't swallow
the crumb.

Separation.
I see
earth dried-up,
although it's crying
from the cracks and rifts.

1969

The throe lives
in the throat.
Literally . . .
Pain belongs to
no one alone,
and to whom
would
going without be strange?

Their words, whereto?
Whereto
between me and you
the longing?

"At this deserted
place" . . . and this
perturbed one . . .

1969

Take a look at it,
this image of words:

ABANDONED, ABAN-
DONED, ABAN-
DONED...

Now
go invent,
discover something,
erase the faltering—

Look over here, I
continue,
to set dots.
Aban-
doned...

O long time!
O dungeon!

1969

Yesterday (sole
recognizing of self,
sole
losing of self),
today
(the missing),
tomorrow (the loss).

And where is
all this about yesterday
and tomorrow
preserved?

In the Always
made of black,
womb of fire
and of all vision.

There
our stay,
close together,
certain.

1969

Experience!
At its zenith
it perceives you
as an inmost
in the sorrow
of here.

Oh, the sun
becomes beholder
in the grasping of
your cheeks,
temples,
and mouth.

1969

RECENTLY IN TÜBINGEN

The tower there
in T.

"Grant me,
Mr. Librarian,
a line
from your own hand."

But he did not
drop by—
on anyone in T.

Would that time
passed away for me.

1969

Eyes in my flesh,
look at me, he
who stares at you, so that
guise and counterguise
get caught up
in one face,
gazing
in all directions.

1969

The way all
of them went
between air,
opened doors
and shut them,
became frightened
or stayed calm—,
how it was,
how it will be,
so is, so . . .
come!

1970

Is there a song
that brings us solace?
Tell me the song
that brings us solace.
There is no song
that brings us solace,
and there are the beautiful
among those of ash.

"Does the white snow
not melt away?
Snow, you know . . ."

In the sphere
of the teardrop,
o captured.

1970

Take us,
you stark,
you sharp hedges,
so that we

might cling to you,
unsleepingly
regarding one another,
bleeding from the eternal,

from that, therefore,
which is.

1970

TAKE, GOLDEN DECAY

Take, golden decay,
the flower of the spirit, flower of the spirit
to yourself, at a time, where
a laugh laughs, like this
at flower of the spirit.

What emerged there, it
slaughters itself.

Afterward, after
a being split it-
self from being,

love breathes again.

1971

BACK THEN

Back then
in Bethlehem in the hay,
merely a child,
quite common people the parents,
safe among animals
and the mother's hair.

Some kind of light in the manger.
Oil.
Mount Olivet.
He was alone there.

Ah, the middling father,
the God of letters,
forced to love.
Of course that's how
a new eon begins.

When a man is chosen
to be a divine teacher,
he, alone, is destined for

misunderstanding
and misuse of his name.
Bloody the bells
in Christ's millennium.

Savior! Son among sons!
When I look at you,
you, nailed to the earth,
loving it with open understanding,
holy life of the life in view,
the burning candles here
in the frosts ought to please me
for your sake.

1972

Repeatedly
written memory:

Didn't I tell
you ages ago
that we would
see each other again
where things don't line up,
where the pain on
the crust of Earth
would be happiness?

This, love
once again, then, is
like the law,
never again.

Taciturn
after these times,
the unconditional
confession.

1972

You, rider
on your own
bloodstream,

nautical I
that feels itself fade
at the helm,

while
sail and bow
sink into darkness.

1973

That came
from a
child's bed of earth,
so that the while
I had to say: I.

Afterward, here-
after: I made
it through. Why
the flower
stands colorfully,
unknowing, that

would be my question,
if I were still asking.

1973

Ever since I was a boy,
I had a lot of Yes on my tongue.

But God, the nullity
with flowers for hair, says No.

1974

MORTUAL

To lie without longing
in the belly of the planet
hidden lost
for all time.

Far from the slaughter
sacrificed by gods
who, like heaven,
are there unknowingly.

1974

Cloud formation
never gets old.
The sky, the pure one,
is emperor,
assassin
of all faces.

Ah, it ought not
perturb me,
strangled
by the veils of the brides,
Earth, the dark one,
is servant.

1975

Tell no one,
What is unbearably
true,
tell no one.

To have unwisely
become too knowing,
Secretly—when
might this still happen?

Looking at eyes,
eager for eyes
in the shadowing,
I weep.

1975

The measure set
for all effort
by a head
that wants negation.

In his cave
nothing is seen
of man or beast
from a gray and yellow age.

1975

What will sleep forever.
Lust—and
riddling has
learned too much.

1976

Carrion and
butterfly.
Disgust
has wings
and builds a house
in a remote place.

But there, disabling
any latch,
whenever
he wants,
the dark ruler
of any house.

1976

VARIATION ON HERDER

From the beginning
the death rattle
in the shard,
the corporeal.
The songs
fabricated
out of the urge of the heart
are things,
as love
arranges them.

A masculine spirit
stays on land,
where there is also
the question
to smile at:
How, if a
sparrow
were to soar to the moon—
and the result
of zeros.

O vagina hominum,
heart, which has
in itself no end!
On the foothills
of hope
lives
what can
live on them:
a small fraction only
of the whole.

1976

This dot,
called sun,

head,
ray of darkness,

provoking and liquidating
essence at once.

1976

Swallows before limitless
twilight clearing, their
stitch and stitch
through the midair mesh.

I ask the skies,
I ask the summer of Earth:
Is it true that I'm alive?

Then a swallow sews
its way through me.

1976

there are people
    just as
       there are umbrellas.

1978

TRIALS-TRIBULATIONS

today I
met with the realization.

and yet: precipitation.

1978

The word,
hand in hand
with pain,
upends it,

so that
what's turned around
would be
through precise pointing?

Clarity
arises, what else,
unburdening the soul.

Closeness of the origin.

1979

THE TRANSLATORS WOULD TO THANK
LEA PAO AND SARAH HENNEBÖHL FOR
THEIR SUGGESTIONS.